Thee
Almighty
– & –
Insane

CHICAGO GANG BUSINESS CARDS
FROM THE 1970s & 1980s

BY BRANDON JOHNSON

THEE ALMIGHTY & INSANE
WWW.THEEALMIGHTYANDINSANE.COM

SECOND EDITION
COPYRIGHT © 2017 BRANDON JOHNSON
ISBN: 978-0-692-86610-8

PRINTED IN SINGAPORE BY ALSODOMINIE
DESIGN: BENJAMIN WALTON / FOOD I CORP ENTERPRISE

SPECIAL THANKS TO DEVON DIKEOU & ZINGMAGAZINE FOR
PUBLISHING THE FIRST EDITION OF THIS BOOK AND THE
CONTINUED SUPPORT. THANKS ALSO TO BEN WALTON FOR HIS
DESIGN COLLABORATION, LEVI MANDEL FOR HIS PHOTOGRAPHY,
AND THE NUMEROUS OTHERS WHO HELPED AND ENCOURAGED
ME ALONG THE WAY. AND OF COURSE BIG THANKS TO MY POPS
FOR THE INTRODUCTION THAT MADE THIS POSSIBLE.

FOR MORE INFORMATION ON THE HISTORY AND CULTURE
OF GANGS IN CHICAGO SEE CHICAGOGANGHISTORY.COM,
STONEGREASERS.COM, GAYLORDS712.COM, @CHICAGOHOODZ,
@CHITOWNHOODART, AND THE BOOKS *MY BLOODY LIFE: THE
MAKING OF A LATIN KING* BY REYMUNDO SANCHEZ, *ROMANTIC
VIOLENCE IN R WORLD* BY MARK WATSON, AND *LORDS OF
LAWNDALE: MY LIFE IN A CHICAGO WHITE STREET GANG* BY
MICHAEL SCOTT. THESE WERE MY POINTS OF REFERENCE FOR
LEARNING MORE ABOUT THIS WORLD, A PROCESS THAT IS STILL
ONGOING. AND FINALLY RESPECT TO THE ORIGINAL CREATORS
OF THESE CARDS AND THEIR ROLE IN PRODUCING THIS PRINT
SUBCULTURE THAT IS UNIQUE TO THE CITY OF CHICAGO.

In the attic of our house in suburban Chicago there was a cigar box of my Dad's old belongings: a yellowed copy of Abbie Hoffman's *Steal This Book*, assorted pocketknives, pelts of thirteen-lined ground squirrels, and other relics of his youth that I enjoyed looking at from time to time. One object that caught my eye in particular was an aged business card that read "Royal Capri's (Chicago)" in red ink, and listed names: "Jester, Hooker, Cowboy, Sylvester, Lil Weasel." It had stock graphics—a pair of dice and Playboy bunny logo—and in the top left corner the words "Compliments Of." When I asked him about the card, Dad told me his friend made it for graphic arts class in high school but didn't elaborate further. Being younger at the time, around 12 years old, I accepted this answer and left it at that to explore other treasures from the attic.

Later on down the line after moving to New York, I was back home for a visit and crossed paths with the card again. This time I purloined it for a little independent research and quickly discovered that this "compliment card" was part of a larger phenomenon native to the Chicagoland area, most prevalent during the 1970s and 1980s, when street gangs made business cards displaying their symbols, nicknames, territories, and enemies as a means to assert their pride, recruit new members, and serve as general tokens of affiliation. Less intended, but maybe more significant for today is the role of these cards as historical artifacts—not only documenting the specific histories of these gangs and their members, but also the social dynamics of a violent and contentious time period in the city of Chicago.

Many Chicago street gangs of this era find their roots as social athletic clubs, community organizations, and greasers. This is not to imply there wasn't any violence, because there was plenty of that. In fact, fighting other gangs seemed to be half the point—the other half being a sense of protection and camaraderie. Racial tension was a source of conflict, arising as disputes over territory in street-level tit-for-tat attacks. In the late 1950s and 1960s Latinos were being pushed out of Lincoln Park and their West Side neighborhoods due to gentrification and municipal projects including extensions of Univerisity of Illinois Chicago and "The Circle" interchange for the Kennedy and Dan Ryan Expressways. These groups ended up in Pilsen and Little Village on the West Side, and Humboldt Park, Logan Square, and other neighborhoods on the North Side. These migrations, along with a new wave of Latino immigration in the mid-

1960s resulting from civil rights inspired changes by Congress to U.S. immigration policies in the form of the Immigration and Nationality Act of 1965, became a focal point for White and Latino gangs in the 1970s and 1980s. White gangs perceived their role as defending their neighborhoods and way of life from encroaching outsiders, and Latino gangs saw theirs as protecting themselves and their cultures from social injustice in the form of oppression and racism. Nativism has a long history in the United States, with each new wave of immigrants bearing resistance from groups already established. Chicago was no exception, and street-level violence between gangs was in part an expression of this.

But conflict wasn't simply drawn along racial lines. There was infighting among gangs of the same races as well as cross-race gang alliances. The Folk Nation was founded in 1978 by Larry Hoover of the Black Gangster Disciples at the Illinois Department of Corrections in order to control gang wars and alliances in the prison system. This alliance spanned across races, and included Black, White, and Latino gangs such as the Black Disciples, Gangster Disciples, La Raza, Latin Eagles, Maniac Latin Disciples, Two Six, Simon City Royals, Spanish Cobras, North Side Popes, Latin Lovers, Sin City Boys, Satan Disciples, Ashland Vikings, King Cobras, Harrison Gents, Orquestra Albany, Ambrose, and others. The People Nation was immediately formed in response and included the Vice Lords, El Rukns (now Black P. Stones), Latin Kings, Almighty Gaylords, Latin Counts, Party Players, Insane Unknowns, Familia Stones, Spanish Lords, Bishops, South Side Popes, Mickey Cobras, and Four Corner Hustlers to name a few. Both Folk and People names and symbols frequently appeared on cards in the form of pitchforks, crowns, devil's horns and tails, 3-D pyramids, crescent moons, and five- or six- pointed stars. These alliances were respected even more than race, especially as the organizations became increasingly profit-minded through criminal enterprise. By the 1990s the drug trade flourished and while these alliances continued to exist, they could not guarantee peace between members.

History aside, this book serves as an ode to Chicago compliment cards: the hand-drawn graphics, the blackletter typefaces, the outlandish names and clever slogans. Intriguingly cryptic to the uninitiated, learning to read the cards gives insight to how they interrelate. For example, an upside-down symbol or name is a sign of disrespect. Acronyms ending with the letter "K" mean "killer"—so "S.D.K." would be short for "Satan Disciples Killer". One Insane Pope card within these pages has the name "Larkin" crossed out with "is dead" and "G/L's" handwritten beneath, indicating that the Pope's leader Larkin was killed by the Gaylords. Speaking of which, the Almighty Gaylords—a powerful White gang in Chicago during this time period—frequently utilized racist iconography and language on their cards. While these idealogies may have been half-baked and the rhetoric a form of posturing, demonstrations of racial pride (and hate) can't be ignored. Readers are encouraged to draw their own conclusions.

More recently, Dad elaborated on that old business card's origins, telling me his friend had been a member of the Royal Capris and saying he'd probably get a kick out of my interest in the subject. I've since become fascinated with these idiosyncratic cultural objects from my hometown, and have managed to acquire a number of original compliment cards of my own. While some of the gangs in this book are now defunct, others remain active. For various reasons the practice of creating business cards has fallen by the wayside. This book catalogs a selection of favorites from my collection. Enjoy.

—Brandon Johnson

Compliment's of thee Almighty

Future Chicago

Shotgun
PRES.

Topcat
VICE-PRES.

Dave

Savage

Flaco

Sinbad

Chinaman

Silver

Player's

Devoted K·K & G. B. O. Killers

Coyote   Lil Dave

NLmighty   Unknown

            Pope's

Chicago Wonder Chicago kid

INDEPENDENCE PARK

BIRDMAN ~~LARKIN~~

COMPLIMENTS OF *B/ IS DEAD 'P G/L's*

Insane Pope's

LIL GREASAR   LIL CEASAR

God made love, God made pain
God made C Note $, Almighty & Insane

Almighty

Argyle -N-
Lavergne

Ohio -N-
Leavitt

SABBATH
MICK
DEMON
LIL OZZY
STICKY
LIL BUGS
MR. C.B.
DAGO
LEFTY-C

WARLOCK
JUDAS
LIL MALO
CURLEY-C
RICO-C
LIL DEVIL
LIL SLY
OZZY
HIT-MAN

Mk-K
Scr-K

Fl-K
12D-K

C-Notes

ALMIGHTY G-NOTE$ NATION

SCORPIO &   LOMP$ 07
NOMAD
GPT   Lil OZZY
  $OME

Compliment of thee Almighty

O/L C-NOTE$ E/L

L-D-K T-J-K

Lee

Wino

Mr. Bee

Insane
Tokers
of 19th

I-6-K

I-8ᴴ-K

Lil Chico

Hec

Lil Bruce

Lucky

Red

Compliments of Fro
Thee
Monticello & Wilson
Freaks

A FRIEND WITH WEED
IS A FRIEND INDEED

Loebs

Farmer

KOOKIE   CHUCKIE   SPACECAT
RIDGERUNNER   CHICO   IRONMAN

STONED  FREAKS

SWORN TO FUN LOYAL TO NONE

BONEHEAD   MOUSE   MIDNIGHT RAMBLER

Lord Jim

Magnum

Baby-Blue

Axe

Bre

Champ

Weed

Maniac

Stoner

Duke

Buzz

Fry

𝕭𝖚𝖙𝖈𝖍   𝕭-𝕷 𝕾𝖙.   𝕲𝖚𝖘𝖙𝖔

 𝕬𝖑𝖒𝖎𝖌𝖍𝖙𝖞 𝕱𝖗𝖊𝖆𝖐𝖘

STONEWALL   MUGGS   POTHEAD

𝕱-𝕷   SIR HASH   𝖂-𝕻-𝕺

Compliments of: Bodean

Thee Almighty & Insane

UNITED FREAKS
L-C

Hawkeye	Buzz
Pipeman	Bandit
Frymind	Lil Bruiser
Ringo	Shotgun

Black and Red...
till Folks are Dead!

Freaks World...
You just live in it!

"Mr. YNK"

"Thief"

"Lunatic"

"Bud Head"

F L

Gangsters

G-Notes

Nighthawk   Wizard

The Almighty
Logan Square
Heads

Jive   'Lil' Nate
Punchy   Iron Man
Sylvester   Klown   Buck

Lil Marco   Wolf   Ceacil

Member of the

Almighty Insane

KILBOURN PARK

Slylords

Lil Ceaser   Mugsy   Lil Rock

PRESIDENT MR. O-A   VICE PRESIDENT LIL GAUCHO

Compliments of
The Almighty Insane Orchestra
Albany Gangsters

ALBANY SCHOOL

KOOL-AID

OUTLAW

CAPONE

SCORP

LIL-LION

SARGE

LIL-OUTLAW

LIL-BUZZ

SIMON-CITY

R

Ain't no pity in
Simon-City

K-K   2-K

GLK

ROYALS

MAD-DOG

SHORTY

SPANKY

GRAN-PA

BABY-FACE

DUBA

SCARY-C

DEVIET

THERE IS NO PITY IN SIMON CITY

**CROSS IS
BOSS**

**THE ALMIGHTY
TOUHY AND RIDGE**

**DOWN WITH THE
CROWN**

**TWAT
LIL BLADE
IDS**

**RAT
LIL PHIL
SATAN**

**SNAPER
LIL RAT
MOPE**

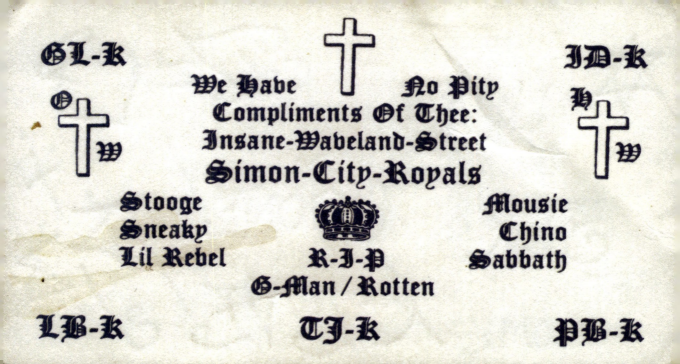

GL-K ✝(O/W)   ✝   ID-K ✝(H/W)

We Have   No Pity
Compliments Of Thee:
Insane-Waveland-Street
Simon-City-Royals

Stooge   Mousie
Sneaky   👑   Chino
Lil Rebel   R-I-P   Sabbath
          G-Man / Rotten

LB-K   TJ-K   PB-K

Campbell-Lunt

Simon-City-Royals

Lil Capone	Lil Dagger
The Professor	Weasel
Sandman	Beast
Sultan	Pyro
Gilligan	Pest
Paz	Casper
Tyrant	Lil Rebel

Lil Satan - Jungle Jim

Sneaky - Lil Joker

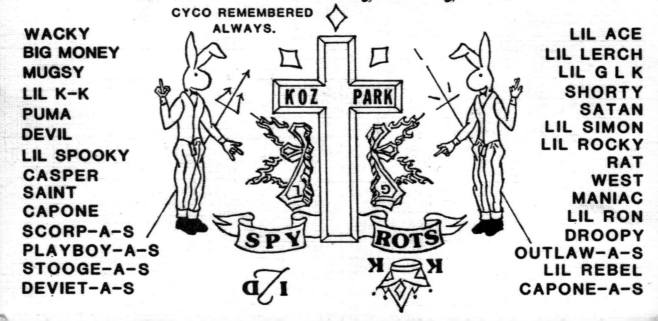

Simon City

C
LIL CAPONE
HIT-MAN
LIL SHOTGUN
SIR ACE
MR. PLAYBOY
LIL SUICIDE
DEVIL
CRAZY G
POLACK
I-2-D-K
PRS-K

W
LIL MAN
YODA
SKID
GOOFY
REAPER
ORCO
LIL ACE
BUZZY
CLAY
U-K-K
P-B-K

Royals

TODDY - N - SPOOKY
R.I.P.

| LEFTY | MARIO | K. C. |
| ART | | VITO |

Compliments of

LOS PISTIADORES

of

17

| CHRIS | — I — | JR. |

Compliments of

Phantom

From Thee Insane Miniature

Night Crew

Latin Soul Killer

L · S · K

Beto Phantom Lil Gangster
Trigger Comps Lil Man

Wizer

Muff

J.C.

Ram

Oz

Chico

Kayo

Drac

Compliments From
Thee Almighty

Night Crew Association

of

45th St. N Justine
Latin Soul Killers

Mustang

Carbon

Puppet

Boner

Healy

Styx

Zepro

Casper

Beto
Shorty

Shadow

Ki Ki
Baby "G"

Simore
Shorty

Andy
Butch

Insane

Un Knowns

Cholo
K-Ray

Kent
Brain

K-P GAYLORDS Rule!

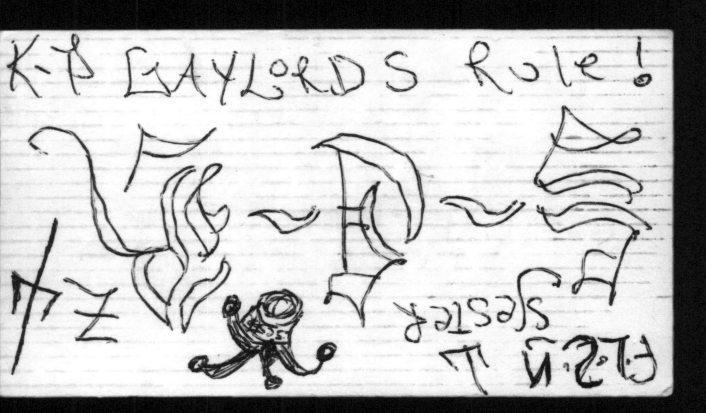

"LIL" KENT
KING PAGO

ZORRO
"LIL"
KING

"LIL"
KNO
GIGOLO

BRIAN
CANE

malo

C.K

Compliments

mayo

C.K

Of Thee

Almighty Gangster

Two ♦♦♦ Six

Nat1on

B.K

lucky

P.K

t-bone

Al

Trouble

Rican

Compliments of
Thee Almighty

Marcos

Smokey **Two Six Boys**

Dabe

of

K-Town

INSANE
SPANISH COBRAS

Junior
Loco
SHOT GUN

Ridgeway
- N -
Thomas

Lil Man
Berreta
Flaco

Papo
Demon
Shorty

Central Park
- N -
Schubert

Baby - C
LIL KK
Bolo

G - K   L - K - K   I - 2 - K

Folks Know

PLAYBOY • PACO • MR. SHY
MR. J • LIL BEAR

P.   P.

Compliments

From the

Spanish Lovers
of Sixty-Third

P.   P.

MEMO • JOSE
ROCKY • WOODSTOCK • PLAYER

Nesto   Toker

Marcos   Noel

Rankie   Rudy

Lando   Mario

Layer's

Compliments

of

Thee

Almighty

Party  Players

of 48th Street

Pepe   Luckie

Stevan   Roy

Sam   Robert

Joe   Speedy

Israel   Nasty

Lover's

Lil Kapone   Neil   Buzz   Lil Mafin

Compliments of Thee
Almighty Miniture

Rican   Marcos

Kool-Gang
of 18th St.

Shorty   Fausto

K   K

Lil Gramps   Lil Gypsy

Shy boy

Compliments of thee

Sin=City=Boy's

Party

People

&

Drinkers

Cuban

Lepke		Lil Joker
Monk		Crazy
Smokey		Chiba
Mr. Mafia		Lil Cunado
Mozee		Mr. "C"
Kidd		Chango
Flaco		Lil Boy
Lil Eli		Ghost
Ziggy		Pancho
Lil Player		Lil Gent
Bruce		Wacky

Lil Lupe   Compliments   Star
Lily   Of Thee   Smiley

Party

People

Chayo   Carmen   Launa
Martha   Crazy-Lupe

Drinkers   Lovers   Fighters

Steve

Compliments From Thee Original Damen Party People

Fly

Phil

Yogi

Loco

Tony

Malo

Frisky

Manuel

Wino

PARTY PEOPLE

DAMEN - n - 21st - HOYNE

VANDAL	LIL FRANK	PEPPY	PEPE
J J	**Compliments of thee**		PHIL
LIL PLAYER	**Insane**		PLAYER
PHANTOM	GET SOME!		MANNY
SINBAD	**Party - People** of 17th St.		RATON
KOOL	SPIDER	SNAKE	LIL MAN

COMPLIMENTS
OF THE
Supreme

Latin Kings

KING TO THE BONE
NEVER TURN STONE

K-TOWN LATIN KINGS

WACHO

LIL TATU

CHICANO

DIABLO

CANO

PONY

CHUCO

PITUFO

LOBITO

LIL MEÑO

LIL MAN

LIL MEX

KYKY

SMALL FOLKS

E-W
SECTION

(DEVOTED
MLD-KILLERS)

future

WOLFY
SPANKY
KUKU
CASPER
RATT
RED-EYE

S ★

L

SMILEY
SHORTY-D
RABBIT
FLACO
K-9
NUCH

Dk come get some Dk

Baby Joker
Tony
Capon

Mr. Tarzan

Baby Joe
Snake
Chago

Villa-Lobos

SDK

Nation

TSK

KGK

Tom
Chico

Big Cesar
Half-Pint

Sucre
Lil Lobo

Byrd

Bear

Compliments of
Thee Almighty Miniture
Villa = Lobos
Masters in crime
Killers of slime
And loving thee fine
Young ladies all times

Salsa

Lil - Man

Lil Romeo   Tony   Mr. Kool   Lil Nick

Wino   Mr. Cobra

Compliments

Kool   of thee Almighty   Nick

King Cobra's

Shorty   of Throop-Cermak   Lil Guy

Chito   Nino   Wezo   Tunco

COMPLIMENTS OF CAPONE

DEVOTED

K   K's

Maniac Latin Hoods

NORTHWEST

SIDE

OF STAVE & FRANCIS
In loving memory of Polaco,
from
Sabu, Huffy, Bird, Rabbit
and
Capone Pres.

O·A's K

G·L·K

H-P T-J

Almighty & Insane

T. Jousters

NATION

K.K C-NOTE$

Compliments Of

Palmer Jouster

Partners

Godfather
Hatter

Sly=Lilmace
Bullet

DIVERSEY—N—CICERO

CRAGIN PAR—K

Compliments of Lil ROCKY

The Almighty

Playboys

P B's

JAY
KNIGHT
RICKY
DOC
Lil NICK

Lil SWAN
GOOFY
Lil MOUSE
SAINT
SPARKY

SQUIRREL   SILVER DRAGON

✝

Thee
Almighty
Playboys

LIL SPYDER   REBEL   WINCHESTER

MEMBER: ___SQUIRREL_____

Compliments of Magician

Thee Almighty Play Boys

Kong Lives

Ron Lives

Sir Pope

Lil Bugsy

Lil Spyder

Squirrel

Rebel

INSANE

ODELL -N- WAVELAND

O
W R's
C

SIMON -N- CITY -N- ROYALS

PBK

Biggie Bat Tavo Capone Loco Carho

Crazy Man Sun Down

Spy Compliments of The Almighty R.J.

Zeke Bishops Bro

Wolf Lil Sal

Lil Lil Rat

L.C.D. Lil Al

Compliments
of
"Sir Sticks"

Munchkin

Serpico

Lil Flash

S D F

Pee-Wee

INSANE
2
DEUCES

4 Z D

Damen
&
Clybourn

Froggy

Porky

Lil Zip

K T O

Thee Almighty
Allport

Arthur
Beaver

Manuel
Pablo
Louie
Neto

Mando
Weecho

Reno
Abel
Bichy
Rafa

Boys
Sal

Filx / AR

ARTNUR
(AS)
Li AB

B·K

Compliments of the
Almighty Devil

L/A

Lawndale

Gaylords

Lawndale & Altgeld

G=Love

REBEL COMPLIMENTS SLIM
NORTH + CENTRAL

WHITE INSANE

GOD GAYLORDS
FORGIVES DON'T !

BRANCH
OF
PALMER ST. GAYLORDS

FROG LIL KILLBILLY SLICK
SLIM

Almighty Gaylords
K-P and L-A

THE KIDD
SCORP
SLY
J-C
GONGE
LIL BUZZ
SIR MAD
SIR HOOD
LIL DAGO
SHRIMP
LIL POLACK
LIL CHICO
REDEYE
SICK NIC
BURNOUT

LORD CASPER
LIL CASPER
RIGHTY
BUZZ BRAIN
LORD POLACK
SIR JAP
REBEL
PLAYER
ROCKER
LIL ROCKER
LIL TOKER
LIL MAGNUM
SIR CHAMP
HITLER
LIL BARON

WIZARD LIVES ON...
SPY LIVES ON...

In Memory of WIZARD and SPY
Comps. Of: LIL SATAN-N- HITLER

LAWNDALE
&
ALTGELD

LAWNDALE
&
FULLERTON

MIGHTY NATION OF LAWNDALE

GAYLORD

MGT. P.W. JRS. SRS.

OUR DYNASTY WILL NEVER PERISH

NORTH & KEDVALE   N/K   STONE GREASE

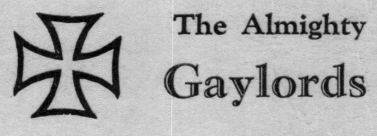

The Almighty

Gaylords

Dago   Chief   Pierre   Lips

Greasers United — Freaks Ain't Shit !

Lil Chief
Butler

Chief
Insane

Lil Batman
Lil Mousie

Thee Almighty
Latin Counts
Born To Raise Hell

Scorpio

Lepke

Chinito

Shorty   Link   Peter   Lil Man   Tony

Compliments of

Thee Almighty Ambrose of 18th C-K-N

Slim   Lil Jap

Lil Blue   Smokey   B.B.   Ricky   Mark

	Compliments of Thee Almighty	
Jimbo	**Insane**	Bugs
Worm	**Twenty-Second**	Duce
Saint	**Nation**	Weed
Tutor	OF CICERO	Papo
Chap		Harpo
Lil Fantasy	K-K-K	Lil Santos

SHY-LAD	OUR COMPLIMENTS	CAPONE
CANO	WE GIVE	LIL DAGO
BIG DAGO	FROM THEE	JOE-ZEP
YOUNG BLOOD	ALMIGHTY	CHINO
RENE		LIPS
NANDO	**"Chi-Town"**	LIL ROOSTER
ELVIS		JOSE
BIG B	**War Lords**	LIL MAN
LOUIE		CANE
LITO CAPONE		S-D-K

Mr. Big   King Killers   Kidnap

Compliments Of
Thee Almighty Baby
Satan Disciples
Of 18th Cal

Alcapone   Count Killers   Lil-Man

Lil Mousie
Lil Monk

Baby Brute
Lil Dragon

Compliments Of Thee

Insane 24th Street

Satan Disciples

Insane To The Brain

Born To Raise Hell

Nation Wide

B·K

Joker

K · K

Indio

C-LOVE

Fullerton
& Kildare

ALMIGHTY
INSANE
ROYAL CAPRIS

KILLER

COLUMBO

RAT

LEGS DIAMOND

APACHE

ROYAL CAPRI'S

SHADOW

COLUMBO   RED

APATHE

KID   WOLF

SHYAN

LAST POCKET POOL ROOM